To:

....

From:

....

Other books in this series

Mother's Love

Love You, Dad

True Love

Friends Forever

The World Awaits

Wisdom and Stories to Celebrate Life's Big Moments

Rachel Buchholz

NATIONAL GEOGRAPHIC

Washington, D.C.

Published by the National Geographic Society
1145 17th Street N.W., Washington, D.C. 20036

ISBN: 978-1-4262-1474-5

National Geographic Society
1145 17th Street N.W.
Washington, D.C. 20036-4688 U.S.A.

For information about special discounts for bulk purchases, please contact
National Geographic Books Special Sales: ngspecsales@ngs.org

For rights or permissions inquiries, please contact
National Geographic Books Subsidiary Rights: ngbookrights@ngs.org

Interior design: Melissa Farris

Printed in Hong Kong
15/THK/1

To my sister,
who's never been afraid
to start any kind of adventure.

Introduction

When my family transferred across the country, I had to move myself into college. Abandoned? Nah. More like orangutaned. A young orang stays with Mom until it's about eight years old. If she's done her job—as my parents certainly had—she can nudge it out of the nest, confident it has the skills to be successful. And only by leaving the nest will it learn to survive. Animals' lives may not seem relatable to human experience, but we can still learn from their survival strategies. We all face wild journeys—new jobs, new schools, new adventures. Hopefully, just like orangutans, we can always visit Mom when things get a little too wild.

Mother knows best. *Orangutans are solitary animals—except when it comes to moms and babies. Females have only one baby at a time and do not have another until the first one leaves the nest.*

Don't just follow your dreams—
Chase them down, grab hold,
and don't let go.

KELLIE ELMORE

Never give up. Wild horses are descendants of once tame
horses that have run free for generations.

We should consider every day lost
on which we have not danced
at least once.

FRIEDRICH NIETZSCHE

Make your own music. Sifaka lemurs get around the forests of Madagascar
with a unique shuffle; remaining upright, the lemurs jump from tree to tree using
their powerful hind legs, which allows them to clear distances of more than 30 feet (9 m).

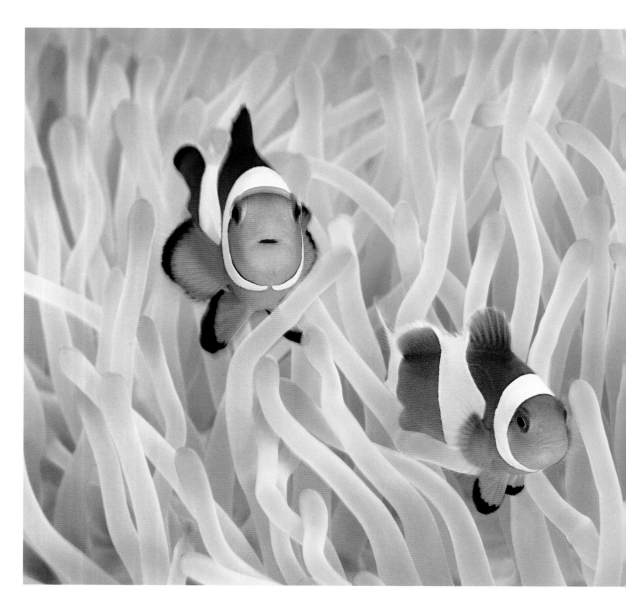

Home Sweet Home

Most fish know better than to approach a sea anemone. Its harpoon-like tentacles deliver a poisonous sting, providing an easy meal for the creature. But where many fish see certain death, a clownfish sees life. Armed with a thick layer of mucus to protect itself from stings, a clownfish has figured out how to turn something deadly into an opportunity. Living among the tentacles, clownfish chase away anemone predators such as butterfly fish and remove parasites through preening. In return, the clownfish has a safe place to live and scraps of food from the anemone's prey. Seeing things from a different perspective, the clownfish has given itself an edge in the ocean.

Make connections. A clownfish gently touches a sea anemone's tentacles with different parts of its body, a sort of icebreaker dance, before it moves in.

It isn't the mountains ahead to climb that wear you out; it's the grain of sand in your shoe.

ANONYMOUS

Climb every mountain. Perfectly suited for mountain climbing, mountain goats have hooves that allow the goat to balance in precarious positions, and rough pads on each toe that provide a grip like natural climbing shoes.

If you obey all the rules,
you miss all the fun.

KATHARINE HEPBURN

Find a true friend. *Tree frogs and bromeliads have established a symbiotic relationship;*
together, these two species thrive in the hot tropical rain forest.

A Rewarding Road Trip

The snowfall swirls and the wind roars around the caribou. Wary of predators like wolves, the caribou use their shovel-shaped hooves to dig through the deep snow looking for food. The herd knows how to survive in its Arctic winter home—but it's no place to birth calves. Soon it must migrate to the tundra, where there are plentiful plants and fewer predators. The journey will be hard and dangerous, filled with raging rivers, rocky and icy terrain, and fearsome foes. But persevering over difficult challenges often leads to something better. Instinctively understanding this, the herd begins its journey.

Put one foot in front of the other. In one year, an individual caribou may travel more than 3,000 miles (4,800 km) as it migrates throughout the seasons.

Either you run the day,
or the day runs you.

JIM ROHN

There's no "i" in "team." *The most social of all the big cats, lions live in groups called prides. Responsibilities are split among the pride, with caretaking and hunting done by the females, and defense of the territory done by the males.*

Adopt the pace of nature;
her secret is patience.

RALPH WALDO EMERSON

*Go with the flow. Despite their large size, manatees are graceful swimmers.
Gliding through coastal waterways and rivers, manatees reach speeds of 5 miles (8 km) an hour
but can, in small bursts, pick up the pace to 15 miles (24 km) an hour.*

Top Dogs

A red fox couple is about to have a litter of pups. They know the ideal place to dig their den would be on the edge of a forest. But that isn't what's available. Instead, they sneak under a porch—hidden from people—where there's plenty of rodents to hunt. Foxes are pros at making their intelligence work for them. As humans have moved into their territory, the clever canines have figured out how to adapt. When they can't hunt mice, they squeeze through fences to find leftovers in garbage cans. And after one fox couldn't find a den, it broke into a football stadium to sleep on the field. By living smart, red foxes have been able to succeed in a challenging environment.

Think creatively. A fox's tail is a multipurpose tool. It can be used like a warm scarf in cold weather or as a sort of signal flag to communicate with other foxes.

Nature has fixed no limits
on our hopes.

BJÖRK

Keep communicating. *Prairie dogs live on the North American grasslands in family groups*
that rely on effective communication. Loud cries can say "Warning!" or "Coast is clear!"

Always be a first-rate
version of yourself,
instead of a
second-rate version
of somebody else.

JUDY GARLAND

Stay sharp. *Sheep have extremely sharp memories
and are able to remember as many as 50 distinct sheep
faces over a period of two years.*

Greatest Generation

It's late summer as a monarch butterfly emerges from its chrysalis. Its parents have survived a migration to this place, where the larva could eat its fill of milkweed before entering its pupa state. But this butterfly, just like its great-grandparents, is different from previous generations. It's strong enough to make a 3,000-mile (4,800 km) journey to the warmer climates of Mexico and back again. And it knows exactly how to get there, as if it's inherited an internal map from its ancestors. The monarch's children—even its grandchildren—won't have this ability. But its great-grandchildren will. Each generation survives so the next one can flourish and make its own incredible journey.

Fly high. *Some scientists believe that monarchs glide on air currents like hang gliders to conserve energy.*

Do what you can,
with what you've got,
where you are.

THEODORE ROOSEVELT

Know your limits. A porcupine has soft hair, but it is usually mixed with sharp quills on the creature's back, sides, and tail. These quills typically lie flat until a porcupine is threatened, then leap to attention as a persuasive deterrent.

Knowing yourself
is the beginning of all wisdom.

ARISTOTLE

Keep it in perspective. *With those enormous eyes, the tawny frogmouth has better vision than most birds—it can even move its eyes in opposite directions at the same time, like a chameleon.*

Leisure Travel

High in the treetops, a sloth slowly pulls itself along a branch. *Very* slowly. Gripping the tree with its long claws, the sloth is in no rush as it climbs about six to eight feet (1.8 to 2.4 m) a minute. But the creature isn't lazy. Surviving on a plant diet that doesn't provide much nutrition, the sluggish sloth makes every calorie count by keeping its energy level down. It even sleeps 15 to 20 hours a day. And besides, there's no reason for a frantic lifestyle when everything it needs is right at hand. Trees provide food and protection, and even the algae that grows in its fur can be used as nourishment and camouflage. Sometimes slowing things down is a good way to survive a stressful life.

Take time to smell the roses. Traveling at a speed of 125 feet (38 m) a day, a three-toed sloth would take more than a month to journey a single mile.

Wisely, and slow;
they stumble that run fast.

WILLIAM SHAKESPEARE

Believe in yourself. *Despite their diminutive appearance, Adélie penguins*
are sleek and efficient swimmers. They may travel 185 miles round trip (about 300 km)
and dive as deep as 575 feet (175 m) to procure a meal.

If you have the guts
to be yourself . . .
other people'll pay your price.

JOHN UPDIKE

Stay terrific. *Pigs may get a bad rap as being dirty farm animals, but they are actually quite intelligent. One pig even learned how to play video games!*

All in the Family

Animals in the wild often must fend for themselves, facing dangerous predators and habitat alone. But not meerkats. Living in family groups called mobs, these creatures have each other's backs. Some act as lookouts, scanning the area for preying eagles and hungry snakes. Babysitters watch over newborns in the burrow, while teachers show young pups how to catch millipedes, beetles, and even scorpions. Then there are the hunters, which bring back food to the group. By surrounding themselves with supportive friends and family, meerkats strengthen their bonds—and their chances for success.

Be loud and proud. *Different meerkat calls mean different things, everything from "Danger on the ground!" to "I'm sorry."*

You can, you should,
and if you're brave enough to start,
you will.

STEPHEN KING

They always say time changes things, but you actually have to change them yourself.

ANDY WARHOL

Know that change is a good thing. *Chameleons can change color for many reasons, but most often they change color due to their mood.*

Taking Flight

Poor ole peafowl chicks. Brown and gray with goofy-looking feet, one is practically indistinguishable from the next. Fresh out of their eggs, they have no idea how to behave or even feed themselves. This new life might be, well, for the birds. But inside every unsure male peafowl chick is a bold, confident peacock waiting to emerge. With brilliant blue body feathers and an irisdescent tail boasting red, gold, and green markings, these birds proudly make others notice them (especially the ladies). And now that they're all grown up, these testy birds bow down to nothing. All it took was a little time and patience for the peacock that was already inside to come flying out of the scared little chick.

Strut your stuff. The feathers in a peacock's train can be five feet (1.5 m) long and ten feet (3 m) wide when fully fanned.

And whoever is happy
will make others happy too.

ANNE FRANK

Stay young at heart. *The ghostly looking Mexican axolotl retains some of its larval features for life, including its feathery pink external gills.*

Don't pass it by—
the immediate, the real,
the only, the yours.

HENRY JAMES

Stay curious. *Sharing a name and a habitat with their larger, black-and-white distant relatives,*
red pandas are most active at night and the hours around dusk and dawn.

The Cutting Edge

Someone forgot to tell the leaf-cutter ant that small creatures are supposed to be weak. At most one-half inch (1.3 cm) long, leaf-cutter worker ants can carry leaves that weigh more than 50 times their body weight—that's like a human carrying more than four tons! Their sawtooth-like jaws are strong enough to cut through leather, vibrating about a thousand times a second. Even the tiniest leaf-cutters are not to be messed with as they ride on the backs of workers to fight off parasitic flies. Many creatures are stronger than they look. But they only truly succeed when they attempt something that no one thinks they can do.

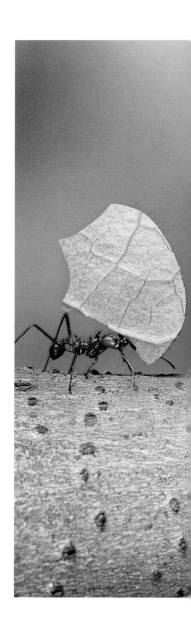

Be in it for the long haul. Leaf-cutter ants will travel more than three football fields to find their booty.

Why not go out
on a limb? Isn't that
where the fruit is?

FRANK SCULLY

Have some fun. *Lar gibbons use a dramatic form of
locomotion, called brachiating, to move through the jungle
at up to 35 miles (56 km) an hour, bridging gaps as wide as
50 feet (15 m) with a single swinging leap.*

Determine that the thing can
and shall be done, and then . . .
find the way.

ABRAHAM LINCOLN

Go to extremes. *Living in the harsh climate of Russia's eastern birch forests,
Siberian tigers are the largest of all wild cats and are renowned for their power and strength.*

Amazing Race

As soon as sea turtle hatchlings break free from their shells, they start an incredible but sometimes frightening journey. Starting with a nighttime race across the beach, these hatchlings must avoid predators such as crabs and seagulls hoping for a meal. To find the water's edge, the turtles follow cues such as the slope of the beach, the natural light from the ocean, and the white crests of the waves. But the ocean's edge does not guarantee safety. The hatchlings must endure a multi-day "swimming frenzy" to get into deep waters, away from predators. If they survive, they have the open ocean to explore, an uncharted but amazing adventure.

Take the plunge. A green sea turtle can hold its breath for five hours, during which time its heart beats only once every five minutes.

It's good to have an
end to journey toward;
but it's the journey that
matters, in the end.

URSULA K. LE GUIN

Be versatile. Fennec foxes have long, thick, soft fur coats with
a woolly undercoat. This insulates them during cold nights
and protects them from the desert sun during the day.

Nothing is impossible,
the word itself says, "I'm possible!"

AUDREY HEPBURN

Go the distance. *Tundra swans breed in the Arctic and winter in North America,*
flying some 4,000 miles (6,400 km) round trip between their distant habitats.

Instant Message

Humans have no idea what all those dolphin squeaks, whistles, and clicks mean. But they make perfect sense to bottlenose dolphins. Whether they're telling each other that a buffet of fish is prime for the picking, warning the group to steer clear of a nearby shark, or calling each other by name, dolphins understand that to talk to each other is to survive. But it's not just vocal communication. They rub fins to say hello and slap their tail to tell another to back off. By communicating clearly, these marine mammals are able to thrive in their world—and with each other.

Say my name. A baby bottlenose dolphin creates its own signature whistle that other dolphins will call it by; it'd be like a human baby naming itself.

Hide not your talents,
they for use were made,
What's a sundial in the shade?

BENJAMIN FRANKLIN

Show your strength. *Undoubtedly, one of the quirkiest sights in nature is the gangly retreat of an Australian frilled lizard. When it feels threatened, it rises on its hind legs, opens its yellow-colored mouth, unfurls the colorful, pleated skin flap that encircles its head, and hisses.*

Knowledge comes,
but wisdom lingers.

ALFRED LORD TENNYSON

Make time to roam. *African elephants roam over great distance as they forage for the large quantities of food required to sustain their massive bodies. The largest land animal on Earth can consume up to 300 pounds (136 kg) a day.*

Talent Show

Puffins might be nicknamed "clowns of the sea," but their talents go way beyond comedy. These little seabirds show off amazing flying, diving, swimming, and fishing skills. To feed their pufflings, they'll make several trips out to sea every day, flying at about 55 miles (88 km) an hour. Their wings become flippers as they dive up to 200 feet (61 m) to chase after herring and sand eels. Each trip, a puffin carries about ten fish back in its beak, and it will have made an average of 276 dives per day. Exhausting? Maybe. But everyone has something they're good at. It's identifying those talents and being willing to use them that brings success—even if you have a funny-looking orange beak.

Can't stop, won't stop. Atlantic puffins can flap their wings up to 400 times a minute.

Like all explorers,
we are drawn to discover
what's out there without knowing yet
if we have the courage to face it.

PEMA CHÖDRÖN

*Leave room to grow. Even though it starts out a small hatchling,
a Nile crocodile is Africa's largest crocodilian. These primordial beasts reach
an average size of 16 feet (5 m) and weight of 500 pounds (225 kg).*

The strongest of all
warriors are these two—
Time and Patience.

LEO TOLSTOY

Make time for R&R. Polar bears often sleep for seven
to eight hours at a time and are also known to nap.

Spot Check

Sensing danger, a helpless white-tailed fawn drops to the ground. A cougar is stalking nearby, looking for easy prey. But crouched on the forest floor, the young deer is hidden from danger. Born with hundreds of white spots, the fawn's markings help it blend in with its environment and camouflage it from predators. But it can't stay a fawn forever, protected from life. In three to four months, it will start losing its spots. As an adult, it must learn how to live without the protective markings and develop its own survival skills, such as 30-mile (48 km)-an-hour sprints. Growing up may mean losing the protection of youth, but it also means independence and standing strong.

Know when to blend in. _Fawns are born without a scent, which—along with their spots—helps them hide from predators._

Do your thing
and don't care if they like it.

TINA FEY

Stick your neck out. *Giraffes use their height to good advantage and munch on leaves and buds in treetops that few other animals can reach (acacias are a favorite).*

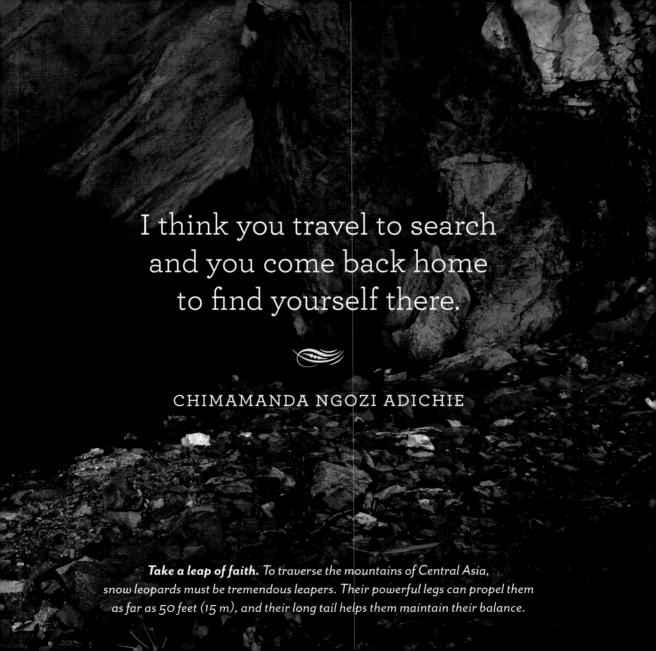

I think you travel to search
and you come back home
to find yourself there.

CHIMAMANDA NGOZI ADICHIE

Take a leap of faith. To traverse the mountains of Central Asia,
snow leopards must be tremendous leapers. Their powerful legs can propel them
as far as 50 feet (15 m), and their long tail helps them maintain their balance.

Earning Their Stripes

The rains have moved on, and so must the zebra herd. Following the storms during the dry season is the only way they can ensure they have enough grass to graze on, so about 200,000 zebras begin their 300-mile (480 km) journey. It will be dangerous; lions, hyenas, and cheetahs will stalk them the entire way. There is strength in numbers, however, and their stripes help confuse predators. Still, surviving the journey is never guaranteed. But there are no shortcuts. The zebras have been making this same migration for thousands of years and know the long way is the only way that leads to a better life.

Stand out from the crowd. Each zebra's stripe pattern is unique, like a human fingerprint.

Be—don't try to become.

OSHO

Be adaptable. *Highland cattle are native to the Scottish Highlands, but they are equipped to handle many climates and terrains. Found from central Europe to Canada, they have a distinctive coat that gives them protection from cold winters, and their diet is not discriminating.*

It's no use going
back to yesterday,
because I was
a different person then.

LEWIS CARROLL

Speak up. Orcas make a wide variety of communicative
sounds, and each pod has distinctive noises that
its members recognize even at a distance.

Illustrations Credits

Enjoy More Stories About Life and Love From the Animal Kingdom

Warm, witty, and sure to bring an instant smile, these endearing little books are the perfect way to show someone you care.

AVAILABLE WHEREVER BOOKS ARE SOLD

nationalgeographic.com/books

NATIONAL GEOGRAPHIC

Like us on Facebook: Nat Geo Books

Follow us on Twitter: @NatGeoBooks